Spiritual Friendship
Darkness and Light

by Ronda Chervin, Ph.D.

St. Paul Books & Media

Library of Congress Cataloging-in-Publication Data

Chervin, Ronda.
  Spiritual friendship : darkness and light / Ronda Chervin.
    p.   cm.
  ISBN 0-8198-6892-2
  1. Spiritual life—Catholic authors.   2. Friendship—Religious
aspects—Christianity.   I. Title.
BX2350.2.C4948   1992
241'.676—dc20   92-9890
                                                          CIP

Printed and published in the U.S.A. by St. Paul Books & Media
50 St. Paul's Avenue, Boston, MA 02130

St. Paul Books & Media is the publishing house of the Daughters of St. Paul, an international congregation of women religious serving the Church with the communications media.

1 2 3 4 5 6 7 8 9   99 98 97 96 95 94 93 92

Contents

Invitation

We all desperately long to be loved and understood. It is a foretaste of heaven when we look into the eyes of another and it happens: my beloved is beautiful and I, too, am beautiful in the eyes of one who loves me.

Then all is light, a release from the burdens of our troubled existence, freedom from the heaviness of self-disgust. Yet night lies in waiting; the darkness of loss, rejection, possessiveness cast their shadows even on the most promising of human loves. Only God's light can banish this darkness. But often it is God himself who brings the "not now," "not that way," or "nevermore."

I am writing this book in the light that has overcome the darkness, yet with fear and trembling, for my encounters in this realm have often been disappointing, sometimes dreadful.

On the joyful side, I will tell of times of beauty in my own life; of the happiness others have described; of the exquisite bondings of:

Mary and Joseph
Mary Magdalene and Christ
Jerome and Paula
Ambrose and his brother Satyrus

Augustine and Monica
Benedict and Scholastica
Aelred and friends
Clare and Francis of Assisi
Elizabeth of Hungary and her husband Louis of
    Thuringia
Bernard of Clairvaux and his brother
Beatrice and Dante
Catherine of Siena and Raymond of Capua
Teresa of Avila and John of the Cross and Gracian
Rose of Lima and Martin of Porres
Jane of Chantal and Francis of Sales
Elizabeth Seton and Antonio Filicchi

On the sorrowful side, I will tell of sufferings, my own and those of others; of the warnings of the saints.

A line here and there may suggest a precise reference. Is it a betrayal of confidence? Not so. The data is so vast, the themes are so common, that my book might have been entitled *Everyman/woman!*

In this preface I want to express my gratitude to those whose love for me has truly been a foretaste of heaven, and also to those whose wounding of me has thrust me into the arms of the wounded One. I pray: Jesus, King of Love, be present to me and to my readers as healing and hope.

Acknowledgments

Excerpts from *Spiritual Friendships* by St. (Abbot) Aelred of Rievaulx', translation by Sr. M. Eugenia Laker, SSND, with an introduction by Douglass Roby. Used with permission of Cistercian Publications, Kalamazoo, Michigan.

Excerpts from *Introduction to the Devout Life* by St. Francis de Sales, translation by John K. Ryan, translation copyright © 1950 by Harper & Brothers. Used by permission of Doubleday, a division of Bantam Doubleday Dell Publishing Group, Inc. Also used with permission of the Society for the Propagation of the Faith.

Excerpts from *Man and Woman* by Dietrich von Hildebrand. Used with permission of Franciscan Herald Press, Chicago, and Dr. Alice von Hildebrand, widow of Dietrich von Hildebrand.

Excerpt from *The Ascent to Truth* by Thomas Merton, copyright © 1951 by The Abbey of Our Lady of Gethsemane and renewed 1979 by The Trustees of the Merton Legacy Trust, reprinted by permission of Harcourt Brace Jovanovich, Inc., Orlando, FL.

Excerpt from *Edith Stein: A Biography* by Waltraud Herbstrith, translated by Fr. Bernard Bonowitz. Copyright © 1971 by Verlagsgessellschaft Gerhard Kaffke mbh,

Used with permission of St. Bede's Publications, Petersham, MA.

Excerpts from *The Embrace of the Soul* and *Reflections* by Charles Rich. Used with permission of St. Bede's Publications, Petersham, MA.

Excerpt from *The Letters of Elizabeth Seton,* Archives of St. Joseph's Provincial House, X, 10, Seton to Filicchi, Winter 1805-6.

Excerpt from *Studies in Formative Spirituality*, Pittsburgh, PA: "Toward Christian Realism in the Consecration of Sexuality in Celibate Love," by Most Rev. Alfred C. Hughes, STD. Used with permission of author and publisher.

CHAPTER 1

Varieties of
Spiritual Friendship

"That you, being rooted and grounded in love, may have power to comprehend with all the saints what is the breadth and length and height and depth..." (Ephesians 3:17-18).

Spiritual friendship comes in many forms: brother and sister, parent and child, husband and wife, male or female companions. Both may be single, married, consecrated, or any combination of these. Such bonds, universal in the history of humankind, are given different names according to the theme of the relationship: master-disciple, soul-friends, companions on the way. A Celtic proverb proclaims that "anyone without a soul-friend is a body without a head." Aristotle thought that real friends were one soul in two bodies.

There is an "all-light" variety of friendship that comes with a rapport in the Spirit. There is a mutual delight in God and each other where everything proceeds in a natural way—what Goethe called an "elective affinity." Here there are no great ups and downs. Warm caring develops gradually and gently into deep union. "We meet life together hand in hand," as von Hildebrand expressed the nature of such friendships.[1] They are grounded in realism. There is gratitude for one another's gifts, a humorous assessment of shortcomings, good advice when needed, and at high points the most nourishing experience of union.

Mother Mary Clare Vincent, OSB, describes this type of friendship when she writes: "We know from the New Testament that Christ had many friends—the apostles, Lazarus, the holy women.... From this we can conclude that human friendships are not only important in our journey to God, they are necessary. Whoever has had no friends will have a warped view of life, of God and neighbor. Encounter with others is the way we realize ourselves and can fulfill our destiny as human beings called to union with God and peace with one another. Even Christ himself needed friends to satisfy his human need for existential communion with others."[2]

The scene of the Last Supper reveals Christ's great desire to share his supernatural secrets with his friends, for friends are to be one heart and soul. Early in the writings of the Fathers we find this theme emphasized. St. Ambrose spoke of a friend as a second self, from whom there is nothing to fear.[3]

Perhaps St. Augustine was especially attracted to his mentor Ambrose because of the esteem Ambrose had for friendship. Even before his conversion, Augustine had a natural leaning toward companionship and a great gift of friendship. In his youthful days, he roamed about with a wild gang. Later he formed deep bonds with other seekers of truth, and when his closest friend died at an early age, he was inconsolable. When Augustine was on the verge of becoming Catholic, his ties with others were so strong he envisaged starting a monastic community of scholars. This group eventually became the forerunner of the circle of seminarians and priests with whom he lived when he was a bishop. A man described by Van Der Meer, one of his biographers, as everlastingly hungry for human communication, he loved to gather his friends around him, and when he had left his study, he was never alone for a moment.

Augustine's relationship with his mother, stormy when he was a rebel, became sublime once he converted and decided on the celibate life. Just before Monica's death, God granted them a joint mystical experience.

Quite different is the rhythm of another kind of intense spiritual friendship. Here sweet liking swiftly moves into passionate love. Need can become overwhelming. The bliss of union alternates with the terror of loss. The pull toward sin can be like quicksand and the salvation from it miraculous.

Abbot Aelred of the twelfth century[4] sheds light on this reality. He declares that friendship is marked with these features: attraction, intention and fruition. "But since man is corrupt, it is possible for each of these three parts of love to be defective; man can be attracted to the wrong object, can decide to pursue that which he knows is wrong, and can enjoy created goods incorrectly.... Then (love) becomes cupidity."[5] Instead a genuine friendship should "begin in Christ, continue in Christ, and be perfected in Christ...."[6] "One ought to lay a solid foundation for spiritual love itself...so that those who are mounting straight up to its higher levels may not neglect or go beyond its foundation, but observe the greatest caution."[7]

In such unhappy loves all goes from dark to darker. In grace-filled ones, the agony is but a prelude to enduring fruitful closeness: two souls become one. Often, though, many seasons pass before peace prevails. Discernments wobble between yes and no as God and Satan seem to vie for dominion. At the end of such purgatorial struggles, there is wonder. Is spiritual friendship a foretaste of heaven or hell?

Delineating stages in spiritual friendship has helped me and others to bring such experiences into the light of Christ. I do not think of the sequence of these stages as fixed or inevitable, only common and well-known. I have called them the following: *attraction, rejection or mutuality, enchantment* and *union*.

CHAPTER 2

Attraction
Stage One

"Where two or three are gathered in my name, there am I in the midst of them" (Matthew 18:20).

It would be impossible for me to count the number of good, loving, spiritual Christians with whom God has brought me into association. Every day, the sight of fifty or so Catholics at my parish church is an abiding sign of the power of Christ in the Eucharist to draw around himself a circle of friends. There we are, centering ourselves in him, listening to his word, seeing him symbolically die and rise, and then being united with him as our divine Lover.

Yet only a few of these faithful who share the profoundest religious values with me are close friends. Strange? Not really. Attraction is a mystery. Someone with less in common may have a voice with an especially appealing timbre, or a laugh that never fails to break through the cobwebs, or a way of becoming peaceful which I envy and want to be near, hoping that by osmosis I might also become more at peace.

So, besides general spiritual attraction, there also

must be some *individual* affinity. Otherwise, there would be no distinction between the love of neighbor we owe even to our enemies and the special nature of friendship-love. Let us listen here to the words of Abbot Aelred:

> We have a clear duty to love all men, and especially our immediate neighbors. For the monk, this means especially the members of his community. But it is also clear that no one, not even the best monk, can find all the members of the community enjoyable; there will be some whom he must love as an act of will and intellect, without the consolation of being able to enjoy their company. Toward others, however, all things will work together to produce a kind of love which is a foretaste of heaven: the attraction, intention, and enjoyment will satisfy not only his judgment of what is right, but also his feelings of what is enjoyable.[8]

The relationship between St. Francis of Assisi and St. Clare is a wonderful illustration of the power of attraction to change lives.[9] The friendship between St. Catherine of Siena and Blessed Raymond of Capua also provides us with a fine model of how two holy people can be enriched by mutual attraction. The life of Catherine written by Raymond, her spiritual son and confessor, is one of the best biographies ever penned.[10]

I found it rather humorous to read his descriptions of the purely spiritual nature of this attraction. Since for many years Catherine's only nourishment was Holy Communion, Raymond mentions that her looks were nothing special in early life and that by the end she was nothing but "a bag of bones." Nonetheless, the charm of her personality, effusive of divine grace, was irresistible and eventually conquered all who sought to oppose her. Unfortunately

Raymond's vivid biography is out of print. A short description of the friendship between the two can be found in *Friendship in the Lord* by Paul Hinnebusch.[11]

There are many examples of fruitful attractions. But that doesn't mean that everyone we have a special liking for fits into the category of *spiritual* friend. Here is where the confusion comes in. I might be attracted to a person who happens to be very religious. I admire his/her fervor. Yet the magnetism between us may be of quite another nature. Perhaps it is someone's sense of humor, a common cause or geographical proximity that draws me. This friendship may still be good and God-willed, but it would not aptly be characterized as a *spiritual* friendship, for it is not the sharing in the spiritual which brings us together.

Vivacious Teresa of Avila reveals herself[12] as quite flirtatious before her definitive conversion. Later she felt guilty about her laxity in this regard, a looseness that was customary in many of the convents of her day.[13] She also tells of a priest who was overly attached to her, but in this case, God used Teresa's spiritual conversations with the priest as a means to free him from a sinful liaison with someone else.[14]

What makes a relationship spiritual is that its very center of gravity is mutual or shared participation in the following of Christ. There are many forms of such sharing: praying together, talking about insights into the ways of God, reading the same books, working side by side in ministries as varied as social justice, mercy, teaching, healing, helping.

The Imitation of Christ states that "devout conversation on spiritual matters...is a great aid to spiritual progress, especially when persons of the same mind and spirit associate together in God."[15]

Consider the wonderful bond between the reformed Teresa of Avila and St. John of the Cross. Through her guidance John realized his own vocation to the new Carmelite order. He in turn strengthened Teresa in her following of the mystical path, for John as a director knew how to articulate this way much better than she did in her early days. John carried a small portrait of Teresa with him on his many journeys around Spain as administrator, confessor and spiritual director.

I will give more references to the writings of St. Teresa of Avila, Doctor of the Church, than to any other saint because the combination of so much experience and her delightfully frank style make her words particularly helpful. Below are a few excerpts from Teresa on the goodness of spiritual friendship and the problems that can arise:

> For this reason I would counsel those who prac-tice prayer to have, at least in the beginning, friendship and association with other persons having the same interest. I don't think how it is possible that a person beginning truly to love and serve God not to talk to someone about his joys and trials, which all who practice prayer undergo. This spiritual friendship is so extremely important since [the one who prays] has so many opponents and friends to incite...to evil.

> There is such sluggishness in matters having to do with service of God that it is necessary for those who serve him to become shields to one another that they might advance.[16]

Where, as in the friendships described above, the primary attraction is love for the unique way another expresses love of God, friends also find great wonder at the beauty of each other's personalities. They may even think they are dreaming, or, as the Jungians put it, merely projecting their own needs onto another. A prayer-poem I wrote expresses this state of mind:

> Are you real?
> Or did I invent you in my loneliness?
> I touch the rough edges
> and rest assured.

Determining the nature of an attraction, as I have suggested, partly involves identifying the specific value in the person that is the real source of interest. Disappointment, confusion and sin all start with a false estimate. No matter how spiritual a friend may be, the relationship will become distorted if I am drawn mostly to his/her sexual vitality, practical know-how, entrée into a desirable set of people, or even simply his/her human warmth.

The ease with which certain attractions can be masked accounts for the many admonitions against attachment to others that permeate classical Christian spirituality. We are told in the *Imitation of Christ* that "if you place your peace in any creature because of your own feeling or for the sake of his company, you will be unsettled and entangled.... Your love for your friend should be grounded in Me, and for My sake you should love whoever seems to be good and is very dear to you in this life."[17] And stronger still: "Seek to retire within yourself. Love to dwell alone with yourself. Seek no man's conversation, but rather pour forth devout prayer to God that you may keep your mind contrite and your heart pure."[18]

When our motives for friendship are mixed, trouble will come, for love of Christ will always be secondary rather than thematic. The real center of gravity in the relationship may show itself very clearly, or may manifest itself slyly in unexpected ways.

For example, you may find yourself abruptly cutting short a time for prayer because a telephone conversation with your friend about trifles went on over a two hour period instead of the shorter time originally planned.

In the middle of praying together sensual sensations may flood the body, not occasionally as is simply part of our fallen human nature, but often and with compelling insistence. Some have labelled such relationships as "spiritual adulteries," for even though there is no obvious physical sin, the passions are all in the direction of sexual union. Heroic virtue may prevent sin, but a more heroic virtue might mean giving up such a friendship.

Bond,

binding,

bondage,

bound for heaven?

More about this later.

If attraction is caused by a great need for the practical support of the friend, then, just when the theme of a visit ought to be spiritual sharing, I will want to discuss less important but more pressing matters. The point is not that practical advice is not a legitimate part of any friendship, but rather that hurtful disappointment can arise from misunderstanding of motives. If my friend counts on me as his/her main source of spiritual sharing, there will be sadness when the long-awaited session ends with nothing more than advice about tax returns.

In general, when it is the natural strength of the other that is a key attraction, any show of weakness in that area can lead to rejection. Some influential people have been so hurt by being used as contacts that they become suspicious of everyone. "Love is a response to the unique preciousness of the other," as von Hildebrand defined it, and so it is rendered less genuine if my focus is too much on what I can get out of it for myself.

A humorous way I have found to avoid false friendships based on what I can do for others is to jokingly announce in public situations, such as classrooms or workshops, "You know, I love to help people with letters of recommendation, introductions to publishers, etc., so, if you need my help, just ask me and I'll be delighted. Don't suppose that you have to take me out to lunch, because I don't have much time!"

The following is a fictionalized story of a common, contemporary spiritual attraction which developed into a true friendship. As the pastoral associate of a large parish, a married woman with many children, found herself drawn to a priest, young and forward-looking, with whom she collaborated in adult education, prayer groups and Bible studies. After a while, sharing about the ministry led to general conversation about personal events of the past and plans for the future. The priest became a friend of the family with very edifying results as the children and husband gradually became more religious. At the heart of the relationship was the silent prayer of the priest and the woman in church. Some parishioners wondered about their closeness, but those who knew them best could see how the priest's intimacy with the woman and her family helped him to overcome the loneliness of his life and made him more sensitive to the family problems of others.

Though less dramatic, some of the patterns in this can be related to the famous friendship of Jane de Chantal with Francis de Sales.[19]

Jane had been a happy, devout wife and mother. Her husband was killed suddenly in a hunting accident. Her life then became difficult, for at that time it was customary for a widow to seek shelter in the home of her husband's nearest relatives rather than to return to her own place of birth, and her in-laws led a very un-Christian life. God permitted Jane to have a vision of a man who would one day be of great help to her. Simultaneously, Francis, a zealous young priest, saw a vision of Jane's face. It was revealed to him that Jane would one day be the foundress of an order of women he hoped to begin.

When they met, the bond between them was clearly supernatural. They were drawn to the great ardor for Christ that they saw in each other. They confided to each other by letter all their hopes and dreams, and in this way exercised a very real support in the midst of the constant opposition they faced in carrying out their work.

Francis was a man of tremendous personal warmth, and in his correspondence with Jane he developed his ability to express affection in a spiritual manner. A cautious and consummately prudent priest, Francis would never meet with a woman except in public or with a companion.[20] But his letters are among the most charming and chivalrous ever written. Here are a few passages from Francis' writings concerning spiritual friendship:

> Oh how good it is to love on earth as one loves
> in heaven, and to learn to cherish one another in
> this world as we will do eternally in the next.[21]

> ...For the delicious balm of devotion distills out
> of one heart into another by so continual a
> participation that it may be said that God has
> poured out upon this friendship his blessing
> and life evermore. I consider all other friend-
> ships but so many shadows in comparison with
> this, and that their bonds are but chains of glass
> or jet in comparison with this bond of holy
> devotion, which is all of gold.[22]

"Many perhaps may say, 'We should have no kind of particular affection and friendship, because it occupies the heart, distracts the mind and begets envy.' They are mistaken in their counsel. They have seen in the writings of many holy and devout authors that particular friendships and extraordinary affections are of infinite prejudice to persons in the religious life. They therefore imagine that it is the same with regard to the rest of the world; but there is a difference. In the well-ordered monastery the common design of all tends to true devotion. Hence, it is not requisite to make these particular communications, lest by seeking among individuals for that which is common to the whole, they should fall from particularities to partialities. But for those who dwell in the world, and desire to embrace true virtue, it is necessary to unite themselves together by a holy and sacred friendship. By this means they encourage, assist, and conduct one another to good deeds. Those who walk on level ground do not need to lend one another a hand, while they that are on a rugged and slippery road hold one to the other in order to walk more securely. So also they who are in religious orders stand in no need of particular friendships, but they that are in the world have need of them, to secure and assist one another amidst the many dangerous passages through which they are to pass. In the world all are not directed by the same views or actuated by the same spirit. We must, therefore, separate ourselves and contract friendships according to our several purposes. This particularity causes no other division except that which obtains between good and evil, sheep and goats, bees and hornets. This is a necessary distinction."[23]

St. Francis de Sales makes the comparison between friendships in the world and in religious orders. I have sometimes witnessed wonderful examples of love within the consecrated religious life, but there can certainly be a danger of such bonds becoming too exclusive. You may have read of the fierce conflicts that took place in the Carmel where St. Therese of Lisieux lived.

Sometimes a common interest in an area of spirituality or theology or literature can lead to a friendship that gradually leaves out others whose company begins to seem dull and insipid by comparison. Noticing how engrossed the two are in each other, former friends may feel they cannot break into the "magic circle." The two who are so interlocked by their attraction to each other may find that during prayer time they shift slowly from absorption in God to efforts to remember or write down prayer experiences that they can share with their friend. Slowly others come to perceive them less as spiritual guides than as interesting people whom they watch to see where such friendship leads.

I keep repeating the word "slowly" in this description, because the negative side of the friendship usually does not show itself immediately but rather gradually; the growing intimacy will seem very promising rather than subtly dangerous. Becoming aware of the problem need not lead to estrangement, however, for once the difficulties are detected, greater balance can be sought to avoid distancing oneself from others in the community. This must not be achieved in an artificial manner, as in purposely rationing out equal time, yet still impatiently awaiting the time to be alone. There must be a happy, full responsiveness to others, and trust that the special sharing with one's chosen friend will find its own time.

Some interesting examples of similar problems in relationships are mentioned in the introduction to a book of the letters of Elizabeth Seton.[24] In founding her community Elizabeth was inspired by the friendship and advice of a certain beloved priest. When the order came under the authority of others, many thought that the degree of intensity of Mother Seton's dependence on this priest was unsuitable and could become divisive. Quite put out about it in the beginning, Elizabeth Seton came to understand that those who did not have any special rapport with her spiritual friend would have felt left out in having him as their director.

Another friend worried about the seeming "idol-worship" in Elizabeth's love for her eldest daughter who lived with her at the school. To those near her she seemed continually preoccupied that her daughter might exhibit some all-too-human behavior that would spoil her perfect "holy" image. I found these remarks both interesting and consoling, for many of us who accept the call to holiness as real pass through phases of inordinate dependence or over enthusiasm.

A contemporary quotation from the writings of Bishop Alfred Hughes "Toward Christian Realism in the Consecration of Sexuality in Celibate Love"[25] could be used in self-analysis or in counselling others about cases of exclusive friendships:

> Because our sexuality is fundamentally an expression of our human orientation to life-enriching relationships, we experience our sexuality as a call to friendship. Human friendship in a broad sense is integral to affective, social and spiritual development. Wholesome personal friendship is a real gift. Good celibate friendship is rooted in clarity on the part of each participant regarding his or her own personal consecration in life. Normally, such friendships develop between two women or two men. Often it is within the context of community life. Healthy friendship is freeing and maturing. It moves beyond emotional dependency and refuses to be trapped in a pseudo-intimacy which locks two people into adolescent relationships. Rather it fosters an ever greater movement toward surrender to God and increased freedom for the apostolate. It

is sad to see how some religious can allow an emotional dependence to rob them of deeper life in God or greater mobility for apostolic involvement.

Let us now look at a positive example of spiritual attraction. There was a single man who never married because of a severe disability. He was a faithful Catholic in his practice of the faith and the virtues. However, he hid from others the dark despair that overwhelmed him when he thought of the youthful dreams he had cherished before his accident, and of the fact that there was no cure in sight. He could not imagine what the purpose of his life could be, and he hated being such a burden to his elderly mother.

Happily, he became the friend of a contemplative religious at a nearby retreat house, a man filled with an unusually radiant love for Christ. This priest's conversation revolved exclusively around the beauty of God, the universal call to holiness, and the shortness of time in relation to eternity. He told his handicapped friend that the only way he could endure the bleakness of his existence would be to aim for sanctity. After awhile "the disciple" became as holy as the master. The friendship flourished for forty years.

In our times, participation in prayer groups often leads to fruitful spiritual friendships. Since the participants come to the meetings because of a desire for spiritual growth, it is natural that they have much in common with each other. Sometimes, however, the attraction can be mixed and questionable.

Praying together in a spirit-filled environment is a rather intense experience. Often quite intimate details of a person's life surface during healing of memories exercises.

The solidarity and warmth that result may contrast sharply with coolness in marital life. The charismatic partner may demand instant renewed love from his or her spouse who is not yet able or is simply unwilling to give in the manner so much desired. In disappointment the more emotionally ardent partner may feel justified in making another person from the prayer group into a husband or wife figure with whom he/she can share deep feelings and inspirations. Such closeness may be healing, yet it can also lead to an overpowering sense of unity and the false conviction that divorce and re-marriage is the only resolution. Where a valid previous marriage is at stake the result is disastrous. In a future chapter more will be said about discernment in such delicate relationships. What is important in terms of attraction is to see that what is drawing the two together is not only spiritual rapport, but a much more all-inclusive need for each other.

Sometimes the spiritual director of a prayer group can detect such a problem early on and work with the couple on modifying expression to avoid going overboard. Individual discernment is always necessary.

St. John of the Cross, Teresa of Avila's director, maintained beautiful spiritual friendships with Carmelite nuns as well as with lay women. In a passage of marvelous psychological acumen, he warns how such relations can yet lead us away from the bridal union with Christ, the summit of the life of prayer:

> We have witnessed many persons, whom God favored with progress in detachment and freedom, fall from happiness and firmness in their spiritual exercises and end up by losing everything merely because they began to indulge in some slight attachment to conversation and friendship under the color of good. For by this

attachment they gradually emptied themselves of both holy solitude and the spirit and joy of God. All this happened because they did not put a stop to their initial satisfaction and sensitive pleasure, and preserve themselves for God in solitude.[26]

Such lines could easily lead one to conclude that it would be better to forego all spiritual friendships, for who could avoid any flavor of what John sees here! Yet that was not the conclusion of either John or Teresa.

In *The Way of Perfection*[27] Teresa claims that, in spite of the danger of temptations, we need love very much in this world, for otherwise life would seem unendurable. The best is to love a holy person, but even when the object of friendship-love is only good, and there is mixed into the relationship a natural inclination toward sensuality, this can be purified and made worthy. Yet, we must always love Christ the most and not be absorbed in such friendships, for otherwise we would affront our Spouse.

The prayer-group couple of my example might find it helpful to read about a spiritual friendship that began between two lay people, Elizabeth Seton and Antonio Filicchi. In biographies of Elizabeth Seton,[28] Antonio is described as a nobly handsome and warm Italian who recognized the deeply religious spirit of his friend's wife. Antonio's original purpose in befriending Elizabeth, besides showing his friendship for William Seton, was to introduce Elizabeth to the spiritual riches of the Catholic faith. Yet Elizabeth was able to maintain an intimate and sometimes bantering friendship with him which later revolved around advice for leading a holy life in their difficult circumstances. Antonio was happily married to a lovely and devout Catholic woman. Though he loved his family deeply, he was often separated from them for long periods of time because of business matters. Elizabeth was a widow struggling against the poverty that resulted from the bankruptcy of her husband's business and her rejection by wealthy relatives when she became a Catholic. Antonio and Elizabeth loved each other profoundly. The attraction began with the spiritual and overflowed into love for each other's entire personality.

For a woman who described herself as having an "inflammable heart," such a situation might have been fraught with danger. Elizabeth avoided such danger by forming an equally deep bond with Antonio's wife by means of constant correspondence; by praying for Antonio with even greater warmth than when conversing with him; by seeing him rarely and never arranging matters to make for more frequent visits when he was in the United States.

The accounts given so far mirror many a life-story. They explain why spiritual friendship has always been a perilous experience for Christians: sometimes light, sometimes dark, sometimes obscure.

In the next chapter, we will turn to another stage and consider what becomes of friendships characterized by rejection rather than mutuality.

CHAPTER 3

Rejection or Mutuality
Stage Two

"I thirst" (John 19:28).

Sometimes spiritual love is one-sided. When the admired other is a distant inspiring figure, lack of mutuality is not too painful. Wistful longing may be the only residue. But when the loved one is nearer at hand, the feelings of rejection are stronger. Sadness, self-hatred and despair may ensue. A terrible thirst for reciprocation may dominate the interior thoughts and feelings of the rejected one.

It is against the background of the enriching values of mutuality that we can best understand why the loss of such joy is a terrible cause of suffering. So, this chapter will contain a description of the growth in grace that comes when attraction moves into mutuality, as well as the depths that rejection can reach, with some additional thoughts about how we might be healed in such times of hurt.

It is only when our love is returned that we can give freely of ourselves. Otherwise, the other is somewhat closed—like a beautiful wall against which the ball of our emotions ricochettes with no effect.

When the door is open, then love flows freely back and forth. It is such an unusual gift to be completely understood in our spiritual longings, in our troubling problems.

Religious novels such as *Mary* by Sholem Asch give a glimpse of what the closeness of Mary and Joseph must have been like. What a gift of God for Mary to have Joseph prepared by God to understand her unique role in the history of salvation. I think of Mary and Joseph as perfect intercessors for us as we seek to live out spiritual friendships exactly in the manner of God's choosing.

A monk once said that in the beginning of the spiritual life we need to see our own yearnings mirrored in the personalities of others. Later on, a glance at the face of Christ will suffice. For some this may be true, but for most of us Christ comes not only by himself; he also wishes us to continue to find him in the faces of others. After all, we are preparing for eternity, and eternity with Christ is not, as the pagan sage Plotinus thought, "the alone to the alone," but rather a kingdom of love in a new heaven and a new earth. Charles Rich, author of *The Embrace of the Soul: Meditations on the Song of Songs,*[29] and one of my closest spiritual friends, believes that since we do not enjoy the complete possession of God while on earth, we need others to help assuage our loneliness.

Since many spiritual directors view pride as the cause of remoteness from others in an attempt to "do it alone," it is important to bring to witness here the many great saints who speak of the importance of the mutuality of growing spiritual friendships.

St. Augustine, whose friendships with others meant so much before his conversion, was no less eager for intimate sharing after he had found the King of love. Even when he was most overburdened as Bishop of Hippo, he would find time each day for friendly converse with the priests who gathered around him at his Catholic academy.

His house was always open, and he wanted to discuss with others whatever was on his mind. He considered that because all the priests of his house shared the same spiritual goals, this love of heavenly things led also to the sharing of human matters.

I have often perceived how difficult it is to discuss even trivial matters with those who do not believe as I do about our eternal destiny. One's philosophy of life permeates even small concerns. With spiritual friends, however, I can talk about details and generally find much to laugh about.

St. Anselm was one of those most eager to defend spiritual friendship against its detractors. The great dignity of friendship, he thought, was that, of all things belonging to the natural world, friendship alone would continue unaltered in heaven. Momentarily it can now be experienced as fully as in paradise where there will be perfect friendship.[30]

Elizabeth of Hungary was brought to the court of her husband-to-be, Louis of Thuringia, when she was still a girl. Elizabeth and Louis spent their time together in prayer and devout conversation. They would vie with each other in good deeds, especially for the poor. In this way they supported one another in the midst of the corruption of the court. Their mutual love grew. After they were married, when Elizabeth would stay awake at night, in prayer, she would remain with her hand in that of her sleeping husband.

With her usual delightful bluntness, Teresa of Avila explains why mutual friendship is part of love of God: "a good means of having God is to speak with his friends....

I know through experience. After the Lord, it is because of persons like these that I am not in hell."[31]

In her *Life*, she confides:

> One day I was wondering if it was an attachment for me to find satisfaction in being with persons with whom I discuss my soul and whom I love, or with those I see are great servants of God since it consoled me to be with them. The Lord told me that if a sick person who was in danger of death thought a doctor was curing him, that sick person wouldn't be virtuous if he failed to thank and love the doctor, that if it hadn't been for these persons what would I have done; that conversation with good persons is not harmful, but that my words should always be weighed and holy, and that I shouldn't fail to converse with them; that doing so is beneficial rather than harmful. This consoled me greatly because sometimes, since conversing with them seemed to be an attachment, I didn't want to talk to them at all.[32]

Teresa's need for advice and friendship became greater as the affairs of her controversial order became more and more complex. Gracian was the Carmelite administrator she found best suited to help her not only with diplomatic questions but also with the solace of intimate spiritual love. An article by Kevin Culligan, OCD, in *Spiritual Life*[33] based on her *Letters*, explains how strong Teresa's conviction was of the God-given nature of this bond:

> Teresa was utterly convinced that the Lord had given Gracian to her to take his place for the remainder of her life. She believed that God had fashioned between them a union 'so well done,

and the knot was so tightly tied, that only death will break it—nay, after death it will be firmer than before, and no foolish notions about perfection could do as much as that' (p. 401). Still, their correspondence, which Teresa likened to her intimate 'conversations with God' (p. 346), was not without its hazards. Often using code names and the third person to protect themselves if their letters fell into the wrong hands, Teresa and Gracian risked the misunderstanding of the other nuns, the jealousy of the Carmelite friars, and the misinterpretation of the enemies of the Reform who would use these letters as evidence against her work. These dangers, however, seemed trivial in comparison with the blessings they found in their relationship, for as Teresa exclaimed to Gracian: 'Oh; Jesus, how wonderful it is when two souls understand each other! They never lack anything to say and never grow weary (of saying it)' (p. 368).

A saint once wrote: "Blessed be those who do not need friends, more blessed than Christ himself!" And St. John of the Cross has this to say: "'Where two or three are gathered...' he did not say: where there is one alone, there I am, rather where there are at least two.... For God will not bring clarification and confirmation of the truth to the heart of one who is alone. Such a person would remain weak and cold in regard to truth."[34]

To turn to other benefits of mutuality, one of the more humiliating ones is the way in which the other comes to be aware of all one's faults. Over and over again we have to see that we are loved as we truly are, and this forgiving love mirrors for us the all-forgiving love of God. One of the most beautiful scenes in the Gospel is that of the scorned

Mary Magdalene kneeling at the feet of Christ. Picture Mary's face in his hands and Christ gazing at her with absolute compassion. The bond formed by such knowledge was destined to lift Mary Magdalene to the heights of sanctity, to be the first bearer of the greatest news ever to be conveyed: "He is risen as he said!"

Mutual friendship often seems like a see-saw. When one is strong, the other may be weak, and so friends take turns being healer or healed. Because our hearts are so well known to each other, we can see immediately when our friend is in pain and rush in with the needed comforting word, the helpful Scripture passage, or the silent warmth of companionship when all else seems bleak.

I am touched by the way Elizabeth Seton and Antonio Filicchi were vulnerable enough to express their need for each other. Elizabeth had just been left a widow, and was isolated by the rejection of most family members because of her conversion. Antonio was in the United States on business, separated from his loving family. Most of their converse was by correspondence as he traveled around the East Coast carrying on negotiations for his company.

Elizabeth confessed to Antonio how anxious she was for a letter from him. Antonio, in turn, lectured her on his own impatience when the postman brought no letter from her. I think the jocular tone of their letters was a healthy instinct to prevent self-pity at being, in a certain sense, "star-crossed lovers." In a letter of appreciation, Antonio wrote that Elizabeth's letters greatly enriched his life.

I have purposely explored the delights of mutual spiritual friendship, as I mentioned earlier, in order to throw into greater relief the deep pain of hoping for such a relationship, only to find myself ignored or rejected.

Having been through several such experiences, I want to express my conviction that this type of unrequited love can be quite as miserable as the ordinary romantic disappointment more celebrated in song and story. I know that I am not alone in reaching points of suicidal grief over such rejections.

Once when I was going through such a trial, I woke up in the middle of a long rest with a vision of Christ's face before my inner eyes. The expression was first that of the person whose love I craved, but then took on more the face of El Greco's famous paintings. The words I heard in my heart were these: "Ronda, didn't you recognize me?" The question brought with it sublime comfort. I realized that everything that I was trying to possess through the love of my friend was superlatively present in Christ, who would always be mine.

Then I also came to see that my sinking sense of rejection was what my Lord experiences constantly because of the indifference of his children to his overwhelming love. The Sacred Heart burns with desire just as our heart does when we seek the love of another unsuccessfully. And is he not wounded the more when the one who rejects him was once much closer?

Still, I argued, how could Jesus want me when I have been so ready even to abandon him, if necessary, out of love for a human person? And he gently wiped away my tears and said, "Come!"

So I confess that, over the years, it has been part of his tender, piercing Providence to open my heart wide with the pain of rejection, that he may have more space for his own rightful throne.

In a pensive mood, some time after such an experience, I became aware that the causes of rejection are usually much more complex and also less personal than I realized when I was at the apex of suffering. Occasionally, people who are spiritually rich are not yet truly open to the vulnerability of intense human love. Usually they have been wounded in childhood by lack of understanding or by sudden loss of parents through death or divorce. In these cases, often the only form of love that the person can receive is one that can keep its distance, that moves very slowly or is available in a crisis. Yet such a slow pace can be unbearable for one who would like to give much more, and might also want to receive much more, than the closed person is willing or able to give.

Those who write about spiritual friendship think it important to try to ascertain at the beginning of a relationship what each person hopes for. Knowing that a person will feel betrayed if he/she doesn't get a letter, visit or phone call every day would certainly be helpful to one who thought one contact a month sufficient. Much disappointment could be avoided from the start by a clear notion of expectations.

Difference of temperament is another common cause of problems in friendship. One who is more of a thinker, an introvert, has deep feelings, indeed, but rarely allows these to show. A more spontaneous nature is full of lavish affection, gifts, surprises. An orderly person may only be able to communicate after all the chores are done, yet the partner wants to be free to call at any time.

Sometimes trouble comes because I may unconsciously remind a friend of a parent or sibling with whom there was a love-hate bond. Tiny gestures on my part might suddenly trigger fear of being banished or overwhelmed.

In view of the many unpredictable factors underlying rejection, it is easy to see that hurt should not result in self-depreciation. Unworthiness is seldom the reason for a flawed friendship. Wisely, St. Francis de Sales wrote: "Others will like you just as much as God decides."

Yet such philosophical reflections bring little solace at the time of rejection. Those who do not go into total despair often withdraw into bitterness. Some rant and rave and insult the one from whom so much was expected and so little given. Those who pretend to be untouched are often not so much saints as they are hardened stoics. Abbot Aelred quoted Tullius as writing: "What wisdom is there in despising friendship that you may...be devoid of fear?...as if any virtue can be acquired or preserved without solicitude.... I would say those men are beasts rather than human beings who declare that a man ought to live in such a way as to be to no one a source of consolation, to no one a source even of grief or burden ... caring to cherish no one and to be cherished by no one."[35]

There are varied ways, as I have tried to show, in which we might be healed in times of rejection. We might get an overwhelming sense that Christ is the Lover whose face shines behind every person whom we would like to have as friend but cannot. We may come to see that it is irrational to attribute rejection to our own lack of lovability. Instead we consider that the other might be unable to love because of his/her own difficulties or deficiencies. Another help can be the solace that comes with the loving concern of others not immediately involved in our initial hurt.

Here are two contemporary stories which illustrate healing grace at work. At the time of a vocational crisis, which stemmed from a bitter feeling by a sister involved in social justice work of not being appreciated by the other women in her order, the sister turned to a well-known priest for spiritual direction. At the first visit her emotions were so turbulent that she could hardly focus on the personality of the counselor. Yet she felt more peaceful at the end of the session.

As their meetings proceeded, she began to notice a luminous expression in the priest's eyes whenever he mentioned the name of Christ, as if his whole self were bowing before an image of the Lord. He taught her how to enter the prayer of simplicity, reaching out toward Christ with few words, opening herself to his presence. As she began to be filled by Christ in her prayer times, the idea that she might have been personally called to the religious life seemed more real and attractive.

Her love for her priest-director increased during this intense time of discernment. It seemed as if he were placing her soul each day in the chalice of Christ's Blood so that she might be cleansed and reborn. Gradually the sister entered into the mystery of the sacraments and her defensive stance began to yield to a more balanced spirituality. She did not lose the desire for social change, but she was able to bring to her cause greater warmth and hope.

For his part, the priest felt his own vocation renewed as he witnessed his friend's growing openness to holiness through his ministry of friendship and fatherliness. A slight edge of cynical weariness which he had noticed creeping up on him in his middle-age also seemed to disappear during their relationship.

Another story, showing recovery from a rejection experience, concerns a single college student in music ministry who fell in love with a deeply spiritual deacon. Finding themselves in the Church praying one late afternoon, a sense of unity began to develop which soon led to conversation, sharing of favorite books, and going on retreats at the same time.

Quite suddenly the married deacon changed his pattern and the young woman no longer found him at his usual places. She was troubled by his disappearance from her life, for she still saw him at the liturgical services. At those times he nodded politely to her as if they had never been close.

Feeling tremendously hurt she finally brought herself to speak to the pastor about her anguish. With tact and understanding, the pastor pointed out the difficulties of such a relationship for a married man and suggested to the deacon that he have a reconciling talk with the woman about his decision.

Happily, the sincere way in which the deacon expressed his concern about his marriage and his attraction to the younger woman, precisely because of her great spiritual and aesthetic gifts, gave her the strength to accept the loss of their daily contacts and, with grace, to eventually attain a deeper interior bond with the same man.

CHAPTER 4

Enchantment
Stage Three

"Sustain me with raisins, refresh me with apples;
for I am sick with love" (Song of Songs 2:5).

Some spiritual friendships proceed directly from mutual caring into the peaceful, tender union I have called Stage Four. Many others pass through an enchantment time of peaceless intoxication, sometimes with the "toxic" element in the foreground.

When this happens, the image of the beloved fills the consciousness in a way which leaves little room for other people. Joy seems to reside only in the presence of the beloved, and all else in life becomes flat and irksome.

Everything we associate with falling in love takes place now, even if the person who is the object of our love does not fit the conventional role, as in the love of a parent for a favorite child, two men for each other, a teacher for a student, or vice versa.

St. Ambrose wrote to his mother that he could not be separated from his brother, Satryus, or even think of him without being moved to tears.[36]

So heightened are the emotions of an enchanted person that all of the sorrows of rejection described in the second stage are increased a hundredfold. That the apparently most beautiful, holy person in the whole world rejects me makes me feel like a disgusting, dishonorable person unfit to walk the earth. Satan works his evil magic so that I believe that the unwilling friend views me as wholly without virtues and filled with obnoxious faults.

Often the sense of rejection opens old wounds and the intoxicated lover feels unable to let go of the loved one no matter how meagre the response. The delicious sweetness of even one compassionate smile a month is enough to keep one longing for the fulfillment of friendship.

Sometimes, precisely because there is so little spiritual self-donation from the unresponsive loved one, the daydreams of the one seeking friendship take on a sexual tone, contrary to conscious wishes. The image of passionate embraces becomes a way of leaping over the insuperable obstacles to spiritual and emotional unity, obstacles caused by the reluctance of the other to enter into a real relationship.

It may take many years of prayer, counseling and direction before a person can be freed from such a tortuous friendship. Fixation on a particular person who has not given love must be replaced gradually by patient contentment with the gifts God is giving and with hope for the complete fulfillment of love in eternity.

When, instead of rejection, there is a mutually intense enchanted love there may still be serious problems to overcome. Most of these revolve around possessiveness.

Here are some fictional stories based on conflicts that I have observed. A sister and brother had always been very close. The brother was the one with spiritual leadership. The sister readily continued her childhood pattern of emotional dependency in an adult spiritual idol worship.

While discipleship is a fine humble attitude, she ought to have developed a realistic estimate of the limitations and faults of her brother so that she could develop her own gifts. Because of her dependency, she became more and more possessive, for she needed to have him near her constantly to find meaning in her own life. In this case, she needs a close bond with another counselor figure if she is to be released from an enchantment that has become bondage.

It is often a sign of over-dependency when the disciple follows the master everywhere and cannot bear to be parted even when it is clearly the will of God that the leader conduct certain ministries alone, or move to another location. Sometimes the stronger one will be able to gradually free the weaker; sometimes another guide will be required to effect the release. The most important feature of the healing is to come to full dependency upon God; to realize that God loves me personally, not only as an appendage of the God-gifted leader. Then I can become a real helpmate rather than an albatross.

Other times over-dependency is reversed. A spiritual leader may find it convenient to be surrounded by admirers who can help take care of the details of ministry he/she would prefer to delegate. Some such cooperation may flow naturally from the helpers' desire to serve. At other times, however, such aid may involve subtle exploitation which eventually results in bitter disillusionment for those who have been "used." A way to avoid such an outcome is to be sure that followers have another source of direction in their lives, so that both master and disciple can be free of unhealthy patterns.

It is also important that those who view their leader as a fallen idol be led to forgiveness, realizing our common weakness and looking to Christ alone as the perfect Leader.

Loosening the bonds can be very difficult. We become so attached to others; it is impossible to see the beauty of another person's spirit without wanting in some way to possess that quality. What we want is not a disembodied quality such as kindness or strength; we want that particular trait as it is incarnated in this loved individual.

I firmly believe that it is possible to participate in the virtues of another in a spiritual manner, but only when we renounce attempts to gain this possession in a physical or emotional way. A woman in ministry writes that her experiences of spiritual friendship range over a thirteen year period:

> I can tell you that there are many pitfalls. And unless everything locks into place just so, it is a dangerous road.... You must realize that every spiritual friendship between a man and a woman has the potential of turning into something quite different. Since the spiritual does involve emotions, it's not that it becomes different; it's that it could get out of hand. The two parties have to be on guard all the time. It can be a very beautiful, satisfying experience, but personally, I think it is fraught with danger. As human beings, it's almost impossible to keep our emotions out of our deep friendships. In fact, I'd have to say, it can't be done. It can only be controlled, and that only through grace.

In his book *Man and Woman,* von Hildebrand asks whether a relationship between a man and woman can ever be fully spiritual yet retain the full ardor and devotion specific to such a bond. His reply is "only when it is a communion in Jesus, from Jesus, and for Jesus. Only through being totally anchored in the supernatural is an ultimate I-thou relationship free of every sexual shadow and yet represents a unique fulfillment of the spiritual mutuality of man and woman.[37]

The words of St. Francis de Sales in *Introduction to the Devout Life* spell this out in greater detail. He gives advice about how to distinguish between true and vain friendships. "Holy friendship speaks a plain, sincere language, and commends nothing but virtue and the grace of God.... Worldly friendship ordinarily produces a great profusion of honeyed words. It coaxes us in little passionate expressions and by praise of beauty, grace and other sensual qualities.... This makes persons falter in chastity and devotion, hurrying them on to affected, wanton and immodest looks, to sensual caresses, to inordinate sighs, to little complaints of not being loved, to a slight but studied and enticing carriage, to gallantries, to pursuit of kisses.... [To] use gestures, glances, and caresses, or speak words in which they would not willingly be surprised by their fathers, mothers, husbands, wives, or confessors, testifies hereby that they are treating of something contrary to honor and conscience...."[38]

Most Christians, perhaps without being able to express it, are aware that there is some law of renunciation underlying a genuinely spiritual friendship. Yet we are so used to trying to possess things in physical and emotional ways that it is a great strain to be deprived of this normal way of intimacy.

To be more concrete, an ice cream cone can be possessed by eating it. There is a sense in which husband and wife belong to each other and possess each other once they have entered into a lifetime commitment in marriage. In a spiritual friendship, there is no possession at all. Two prayer-poems I wrote are expressions of the mystical anguish that ensues as these truths are confronted by spiritual friends:

The endless eager hopeless waiting
is our life on earth
all seeming fullness fleeting.

I want to grasp you...
like a thing?
No. Never will spirit be flesh.

No time encircled being
this awful yearning surfeit
ever leaping over never,
Lord have mercy on my soul.

———

On a mystical ocean of tears,
we swim toward each other—
we, the harpooned of the Lord,
heads far out of the water of the world,
gasping for breath,
supping on clouds—
"Dying yet we live!"

———

Some try for a compromise here. Of course they know that sexual intercourse is a serious sin, but they think they can derive fulfillment from less complete contacts. I believe such a path is one of self-deception. Any touching different from the common expressions of affection by which all Christians display their regard for one another, always carries an erotic charge, distracts from the spiritual nature of the union and often leads to more complete acts.

Spiritual friendship must be an eschatological sign of the union we will know in heaven, which will be total but not erotic, as we are told by the Lord (cf. Mt 22:29-32). Renunciation on earth leads to a foretaste of that union, with a sweet but non-erotic overflow through the body.

One should avoid not only actual touching but also allowing the mind to be filled with fantasies of "what if..." "if only...." As St. Francis de Sales wrote in a letter to Jane de Chantal concerning her great desire to visit with him more often: "We should not want what God does not want for us."

Blessed Edith Stein, who lived as a devout single woman in the world before she entered the Carmelites, was always watchful that those who sought her company did not become overly interested in her own personality, for she had dedicated her life to Christ. She wrote: "Natural love aims at possession, at owning the beloved as completely as possible. But anyone who loves with the love of Christ must win others for God instead of himself, as Christ did when he came to restore lost humanity to the Father. Actually, this is the one sure way to possess someone forever. Whenever we´entrust a person to God, we find ourselves united to him; whereas, sooner or later, the lust for conquest usually—no, always—ends in loss."[39]

For many people, fantasies seem so much less serious than material sins that little attention is paid to their spiritual dangers. In his novel *Descent into Hell,* Charles Williams shows how even ethereal daydreams pervert the soul, for they substitute love which is purely romantic for sacrificial agapic love for an actual person.

C.S. Lewis, a great friend of Charles Williams, reinforces Williams' perception with regard to a matter not mentioned so far, but certainly pertinent: namely, masturbation. Here is a selection from a letter of advice Lewis wrote on the subject:

> For me, the real evil of masturbation would be
> that it takes an appetite which, in lawful use,
> leads the person out of himself to complete (and

correct) his own personality in that of another (and finally in children and even grandchildren) and turns it back; sends the man back into the person of himself, there to keep a harem of imaginary brides. And this harem, once admitted, works against his *ever* getting out and really uniting with a real woman. For the harem is always accessible, always subservient, calls for no sacrifices or adjustments, and can be endowed with erotic and psychological attractions which no real woman can rival. Among those shadowy brides he is always adored, always the perfect lover; no demand is made on his unselfishness, no mortification ever imposed on his vanity. In the end, they become merely the medium through which he increasingly adores himself.[40]

One way to temper out-of-control daydreams is to spend much more time in interior prayer for the other rather than in fantasies about future meetings. The old advice about avoiding near occasions of sin is still crucial. The knowledge that the next encounter will be in circumstances where erotic acts could take place unobserved by others is enough for many people to trigger active dreams of fruition. When in each other's presence, the persons should speak more of relationship with Christ rather than a perpetual sharing of their feelings toward each other. How much the persons articulate feelings of love will depend upon the personalities involved, yet this topic should never be so dominant that Christ is left out or, as it were, shoved into the background.

I am moved to speak of these subjects because of the many tragic stories I have heard in regard to this area of spiritual friendship. In my experience in giving talks and workshops on the topic, I have been assured that most books on the subject are much too indirect in their treatment of dangerous situations. So I am trying to write a book that might help people to avoid so great a fall.

In line with this objective, I am now going to include quite a number of anecdotes about the saints, for we cannot exclude as witnesses those holy men and women who have provided us with the best examples of wonderful friendships. These saints certainly had charismatic personalities to attract so many friends and disciples, so we should not easily dismiss their worries as being distorted repression.

In the accounts of many saints we find instances of great care to avoid any appearance of sin even in the most spiritual friendships. For example, we have the famous tale of St. Benedict allowing himself only a few hours of conversation with his saintly sister, Scholastica. He was, amusingly, forced by a storm to stay the night, to the delight of his sister, who had apparently implored heaven to give her more time for conversation with her beloved brother.

Early biographers of St. Francis of Assisi and St. Clare depict Francis' behavior toward Clare as extremely circumspect. He practiced arduous penance, including throwing himself into thorn bushes, whenever he thought his sensuality might win over his heroic ideals.

St. Catherine of Siena employs the same image as did St. Gregory the Great in comparing the enjoyment of creatures on earth to eating fruit from a tree when it is still green. It is only in heaven that this fruit will be ripe.

Teresa of Avila always thought of Christ as her best friend. "For this love of his...is better than all earthly affection in that, if we love him, we are quite sure that he loves us too."[41]

In *The Way of Perfection*[42] she distinguishes between

the problems that arise between women who are friends, between a nun and her confessor, or between a nun and her relatives. In woman to woman friendships there is a danger of factions and of soft sentimentality and coddling of the specially loved ones. Problems of a lesbian nature must have existed even then, since in another book she proscribes the convent dungeon as the place for those whose infractions of the rule take that form. The remedy for overdoing a particular friendship is to love everyone. In the case of confessors, it is better to choose another one if you are too fond of your own. With piquant wit she remarks that it is not right to confess to your confessor that you like him overly much.

With relatives or with other friends who might visit the convent, one ought not to "use such phrases as 'if you love me' or 'don't you love me?' unless you have in view some noble end and the profit of the person to whom you are speaking,"[43] for instance, to show your love so that you can offer advice and be heard.

And here is her incisive psychological analysis of how even someone extremely spiritual can make mistakes when ardor is greater than prudence:

> The devil plays a trick on the soul. Since it sees itself so close to God and perceives the difference there is between heavenly and earthly goods and the love the Lord shows it, it gains confidence from this love and the feeling of security that it will not fall away from what it enjoys. It thinks it clearly sees the reward and that it is no longer possible for it to abandon something that, even in this life, is so delightful and pleasing for anything as foul and base as earthly pleasure. And by means of this confidence the devil takes away its lowly estimation

of itself. Believing it has no longer anything to fear from itself, as I say, the soul places itself in dangers and begins with splendid zeal to give away fruit without measure. It doesn't do this with pride; it well understands that of itself it can do nothing. It does it with great confidence in God, but without discretion since it doesn't observe that it is still a fledgling. It can leave the nest, and God takes it out; but it is still not ready to fly. The virtues are not yet strong, nor does it have the experience to recognize dangers, nor does it know the harm done by relying upon oneself.

This self-reliance was what destroyed me.[44]

Later in life she was to receive so stunning a vision of the Person of Christ that she was unable to feel enchanted by any human person.

St. John of the Cross has this to say about how to discern good friendships from bad ones: Some people "in their spiritual conversations manifest a certain sprightliness and gallantry upon considering who is present, and they carry on with a kind of vain satisfaction. Such behavior is also a by-product of spiritual lust.... Some will spiritually acquire a liking for other individuals which often arises from lust rather than from the spirit. This lustful origin will be recognized if, upon recalling that affection, there is not an increase in the remembrance and love of God, but remorse of conscience. The affection is purely spiritual if the love of God grows when it grows, or if the love of God is remembered as often as the affection is remembered, or if the affection gives the soul a desire for God—if by growing in one the soul grows also in the other. For this is a trait of God's spirit: the good increases with the good...if the inordinate love increases, then, as will be seen the soul grows cold in the love of God, and owing to the recollection of that other love, forgets him—not without the feeling of some remorse of conscience. On the other hand, as the love of God increases, the soul will grow cold in the inordinate affection, and come to forget it. For not only do these loves fail to benefit one another, but since they are contrary loves, the predominating one, while becoming stronger itself, will stifle and extinguish the other.... Hence our Savior proclaimed in the Gospel: That which is born of the flesh is flesh, and that which is born of the spirit is spirit."[45]

Evidently St. Francis de Sales had much experience—in the confessional and in counseling—with the type of self-deceit which can go along with the enchantment phase of spiritual friendships. Writing about this, he comments that liaisons based on vanity lead to attachments which are "always evil, foolish and vain. They are evil because they come to an end at length and terminate in carnal sin, and because they rob God and the wife or the husband of that love, and consequently of that heart, which belonged to them. They are foolish, because they have neither foundation nor reason. They are vain, because they yield neither profit, honor, nor content. On the contrary, they are attended by a loss of time, are prejudicial to honor, and bring no other pleasure than that of an eagerness in pretending and hoping, without knowing what they would have or to what they would make pretensions. For these wretched and weak minds still imagine they have something to expect from the testimonies which they receive of reciprocal love. Yet they cannot tell what this is, the desire of which can never end, but goes on continually, oppressing their hearts with perpetual distrust, jealousy and unquiet."[46]

Certainly Francis was not hard on his penitents in

order to be easy with himself in this respect, as is evident from this episode from his own life of almost chilling austerity:

At the very end of his life, Francis, a bishop and also a Church diplomat, was often away from Annecy for long periods, leaving Jane de Chantal and her new order often in need of advice that could better be given by word of mouth than by the constant letters going back and forth. Meticulously, Jane would save up all the points to be discussed, including excerpts from her own spiritual journal, for she was a most scrupulous person and found the direction of Francis necessary to bring her greater freedom of spirit. Also, as is clear from his correspondence with her, it was for them a tremendous spiritual joy to be together.

When they finally met at Lyons, not having seen each other for three years, Francis prefaced the conversation with this question: "Mother, we have a few hours free. Which of us shall begin to speak?" "I, if you please, my Father, I have such great need of your advice," cried Jane. "What, my daughter, have you still these importunate desires?" corrected Francis. "I had thought to find you wholly spiritual. Nay, we will talk about ourselves at Annecy. Let us now speak instead about the affairs of our little Order. How I love it, because God is much loved therein."[47]

The biographer adds that his preaching to the sisters was often: "Desire nothing, refuse nothing." When pressed by the superior at Lyons to keep Jane there with him another day, he replied, "Who is fonder of our Mother than I am? I love her as I love myself, but she must needs do the will of God, and go prepare a resting place for me...." (In this way he predicted his imminent death).

There has been quite a lot of commentary concerning this famous parting, for St. Francis de Sales was usually extremely tender and it might be thought that this incident showed too harsh a character. However, it fits in well with an account of a former time when Francis promised Jane that one day she would come to him for direction and he would help her with the last detachment required: detachment from him.

Evidently, the matter bothered the biographer as much as it does most readers, for she speculates that the cause of his seeming impersonal attitude toward Jane on their last visit may have been a test of her discipline, or might simply manifest a lack of balance in one about to be afflicted with a fatal cerebral hemorrhage!

In any case, after his death, his body was brought to the convent in Annecy and remained there in state for some time. Jane spent hours in deep prayer near the saint's body and seemed afterwards to be supernaturally consoled by the wordless colloquy between their souls.

We offer another example of renunciation:

> I could cry out now: Antonio, Antonio, but I call back the thought, and my soul cries out: Jesus, Jesus, Jesus. There it finds rest and heavenly peace, hushed by that dear sound. Jonathan loved David as his own soul, and if I were your brother, Antonio, I would never leave you for one hour.[48]

Twentieth century voices on the subject of attachment and detachment are quite mixed. We find Thomas Merton warning:

> A devout man can form a habit of attachment to some created pleasure by frequently using it in good faith, as a motive of prayer. In actual fact, his desire for the pleasure soon becomes greater than his desire to pray. Without realizing it, he has made prayer the motive for indulging in this

pet pleasure. This can very easily happen, for example, in the case of a sentimental friend-ship.[49]

Von Hildebrand lauds the possibilities of *genuine* spiritual friendship, while Jacques Maritain wrote in his *Notebook* concerning his own choice of a Josephite marriage, that it was impossible to have a mad, boundless love for a person and for God at one and the same time. One or the other must inevitably become more boundless.

My own conviction is that it is a matter of individual grace. Some people are given the grace to love another with intense fervor *in Christ,* and others are called to make a choice, with the human friendships being present but more peripheral.

Overcoming temptations to sexual sins of fantasy or of practice can be partly a matter of growth. John Paul II speaks often about the *serenity* that comes gradually as a victory of grace in the lives of celibates. A book by Benedict J. Groeschel, CFR, called *The Courage to Be Chaste,*[50] has these suggestions for those trying to lead a chaste single life: cultivate a wise variety of relationships among family, friends, and only a few people who could be sexually attractive; have at least one intimate friend; with those who are attractive to you, be circumspect, avoid manipulation, subtle forms of seductiveness and exclusiveness; remember that God has first claim on our love and that active sexuality outside of marriage is sinful and harmful.

Desire for physical possession is not the only kind of grasping that has to be overcome. In marriage, in parenting, in a religious community, at work or in ministry, others who are not spiritual friends often have a greater right to our time and energy. We may wish to be with our friends often, and in a crisis they certainly have a right to our help, but in everyday circumstances, it will be the family, the community, or fellow workers who will often take priority. Spiritual friends should not become possessive of our time. This statement about family life can readily be applied to other communities requiring our commitment: "The living room of your heart belongs to the family."

To neglect family, community or work due to the greater delight we may feel in being with a spiritual friend is to violate the primary duty of love bound up with our chosen state of life. For instance, a priest should not spend an hour on the phone each day with a friend when he would normally be using that time for sick calls. A social worker should not take time out from the care of those in his/her charge to make side-trips to visit a friend. Inordinate demands on each other's time is a sure sign of emotional possessiveness.

Trials of possessiveness of this type become especially acute when one friend moves away. The bereft partner may feel the separation as an almost unendurable cross. Oftentimes such a painful break is part of God's providence. It is a cure for over-dependence. Phrases such as, "I will die if I can't be with my friend," reveal a tendency to idol-worship that is in need of healing through the experience of God's love in solitude. As St. Augustine thought, we should love others but not depend on them. We should not promise ourselves what Christ has not promised. He has not told us that we shall never be separated on earth from those we want the most, only that he will always be with us.

Once, in the midst of a disordered friendship that caused me unbearable anguish of soul, I asked the Lord why he had sent so piercing a cross. Did he mean for me to "bleed" to death? It seemed to me that he replied in an interior way:

"Because I want to give you a still more profound gift, now is the time for you to receive it: peace. Never will you come into my peace if you think that clinging to my beautiful works is the meaning of life. I do not want to take my works away from you, but I am a jealous God. I want your heart to be wholly given unto me so that I may fill it with my peace, so that all your joys and sorrows alike may be full of my peace and not be a tightrope on which you walk and fall and leap frantically through the moments of your time.

"Haven't you heard the whisper of my peace coming closer and closer to you? But you would not come—you are too busy trying to possess what is unpossessible. Never mind; start again in me, and everything beautiful will be twice as beautiful—nay, a thousand times as beautiful. But in my peace you will see the beauty in each moment and never neglect the good for the better because you will be in possession of the best.

"Well, my child—do you say yes?... It is for you to say, but I will never take no for an answer, because I love you more than you have ever loved anyone, and love does not let go."

In view of all the ways spiritual friends can be shipwrecked during the enchantment stage, it is most helpful to have a spiritual director who is outside the relationship. Ideally the ups and downs will be followed in some detail, for otherwise problems leading to sin or to emotional breakdown may build up suddenly, while at the last meeting with the director things seemed to be going along fairly smoothly. Psychological counseling can also be of great value when fear of loss becomes overwhelming.

The turbulence of Stage Three can be so daunting to many that all spiritual friendships are avoided as temptations to sin or as snake-pits of uncontrollable emotions. Yet Christian psychologists question such an approach. They warn against the emotional sterility and spiritual stagnation that can result from overcautiousness. Thomas J.

Tyrrell, in his book *Urgent Longings*,[51] emphasizes the positive aspects of infatuation. Even though it needs to be transformed into a more tender, less possessive love, and even though the vehemence of infatuation may cause others to shy away from the uneasy sense of being idol-worshiped, there is good in the way these fervent emotions open us up to awe at the beauty of others.

It can be false to imagine that the only two choices are complete detachment or fixated involvement. A median term, suggested by the psychologist-monk John Borgerding (St. Andrew's Priory, Valyermo, California), is *transparency*. By this term, Fr. Borgerding points to the way God can choose to reveal himself to us through creatures *or* without creatures. Anything that God made can be his ambassador. God can use a Gracian to enchant a Teresa, or he could demand detachment. God makes individual choices as he brings others into our lives. We cannot program his grace in order to enjoy the security of either plunging recklessly into every friendship which attracts us, or of being totally detached from others. When God takes away a friendship, the principle of transparency means that we can live for a time on God's love alone.

Part of God's individual fashioning of us concerns temperament. Elizabeth Seton described herself as having an inflammable heart. She would naturally have more spiritual friendships than a person of a more practical nature. Yet often it is the romantic person who has the deeper need of solitude.

A director might watch to see how long a period of physical and emotional tension characterizes a bond and whether this strain decreases if there is a lessening of contact: visits, phone-calls, letters. While problems are usually resolved by moderation, there are times when "major surgery" is healthful, if the threat to emotional and spiritual health is serious.

In the somewhat quaint language of St. Francis de Sales, in cases of obviously dangerous loves, "As soon as you perceive their first approach turn quickly away. With an absolute detestation of this vanity, run to your Savior's cross, take his crown of thorns, and press it about your heart, so that the little foxes may not come near it. Beware of making any compromise with this enemy. Do not say, 'I will listen to him, but I will do nothing of what he shall say to me. I will lend him my ears, but I will refuse him my heart.' ...Be resolute on these occasions. Heart and ears speak to each other. Just as it is impossible to stop a torrent that descends from the mountain peak, so is it hard to prevent the love that has entered in at the ear from falling suddenly down into the heart,...with an absolute will determine in your heart and resolve nevermore to enter into these games and deeds of love.... If you can remove yourself from the object of this love, I greatly approve of doing so. For as those who have been bitten by serpents cannot easily be cured in the presence of those already wounded by the same animal, so the person stung with love will hardly be cured of this passion as long as he is near the other who has been similarly wounded.... What must the man who cannot go away do? Let him absolutely curtail all particular familiarity, all private conversation, amorous looks, smiles and in general, all sorts of communication and allurement, which may nourish this shameful, smoldering fire.... I call aloud upon everyone who has fallen into these wretched snares: Cut them! Break them! Tear them! Do not divert yourself in unraveling these criminal friendships; you must tear and rend them asunder. Do not untie the knots, but break or cut them, so that the cords and strings may be rendered useless...."[52]

From the standpoint of modern psychology, it could be added that addictive sinful bonds are signs of emotional wounds from the past. An abrupt termination needs to be followed by intensive counseling or a long retreat to provide an open space for God's love to come and heal.

Indeed, early discernment and help might prevent a relationship from becoming toxically enchanting. It is easy for a good spiritual director to see that the longing to be a saint, or the hope of being viewed as happily married, single or consecrated is not the same as really being so. But usually it is only those who are basically happy in their vocations who can sustain the trials of this very emotionally intense type of friendship. A director should be on the lookout for a certain uneasy fear at the beginning of the relationship. For mere satisfaction in one's vocation can easily topple under the onslaught of the joys of friendships which take place in ideal settings, free from the boredom of ordinary life. The symptom of fear may indicate unrest or unhappiness not visible on the surface of a fairly successful life. The answer need not be to flee from the new bond, but rather to turn to sources of renewal in one's chosen lifestyle.

Honesty also requires watchfulness over the process of friendship as it unfolds. Do we spend more and more time in prayer and sharing about Christ, in openness to other Christians, or is our contact drawing us into a realm of private intimacy where only we two count?

Sometimes we can be released from a harmful bond when a friend dies, or moves away, or when other friendships come to draw off some of the dependency in our favorite relationship. Sometimes it is more frequent contact that diminishes passion. We all have faults and these are more likely to manifest themselves over time than in a perfect setting once a month. But discovering each other's faults need not lead to disillusioned withdrawal. It may be a test where genuine God-willed friendships move into the next stage of union, and the other more superficial ones drift apart.

Before moving on to the beautiful stage of union, let us conclude these considerations with a prayer:

Lord Jesus, King of Hearts, you have made us to be vulnerable and yearning. Purify our friendships of all that is not according to your will, and show us how to live in a way that will image your love for us.

CHAPTER 5

Union
Stage Four

"'You are my Lord; I have no good apart from you.'
As for the saints in the land, they are the noble,
in whom is all my delight" (Psalm 16:2-3).

"[Father], I am praying for them...for those whom you have given me, for they are yours; all mine are yours, and yours are mine, and I am glorified in them.... Holy Father, keep them in your name...that they may be one, even as we are one" (Jn 17:9-11).

The Holy Trinity is the highest spiritual friendship! All of reality can be seen as a dance of spiritual love, of Creator for creation, and of creatures for each other.

Aelred translated "God is Love" into "God is friendship," and he thought of all nature as a sort of society of love. "Suppose we begin with inanimate creation—what soil and what river produces one single stone of one kind? Or what forest bears but a single tree of a single kind? And so even in inanimate nature a certain love of companionship, so to speak, is apparent.... How they (the animals) run after one another, play with one another, so express and betray their love by sound and movement, so eagerly and happily do they enjoy their mutual company.... Finally, when God created man, in order to commend more highly the good of society, he said: 'It is not good for man to be alone: let us make him a helper like unto himself.'"[53]

Even if a reader may never have passed beyond the struggles of what I have called Stage Three, it will be worthwhile to read about the goal, for someday the heart may be schooled to receive the great gift of a friendship free of possessiveness, temptation and guilt.

It is when our love for God becomes all-encompassing that our capacity for human love becomes greater and purer.

In a book called *Holiness,* Donald Nicholl writes that "everyone needs a soul-friend, someone who loves you so much that he will never allow you to stray from the path of holiness without both rebuking and encouraging you.... The inestimable service that a soul-friend renders to his friend is two-fold; first to lay bare any self-deception or lying-to-oneself that the friend might be prone to; second, to lift his friend out of depression by giving him heart, which is what the word 'encouragement' literally means: giving heart...."[54] To these sentiments I add a resounding amen.

In the stage of union, we come to an intense yet tranquil experience. Two spirits, previously distinct, begin to blend. During prayer, together or apart, such spiritual friends can possess Christ at the same moment with ecstatic joy or delightful contentment.

Very often one will be able to know what is going on in the heart of the other, even without words. Efficacious intercession is possible at the stage of union, for there are no more barriers of distrust and fear.

A clear mark of union is an unselfish desire to share the beloved with others. Characteristically, a married person gifted with spiritual companionship outside the marriage will find that his/her spousal union is growing. Previous feelings of disappointment or resentment give way to happy gratitude for the gifts the spouse is able to give. As the soul expands in its ability to read the hearts of others, all friendships deepen.

As many writers have shown, much inner healing comes from such union. As confidence develops in the unconditional love of such a friend, previous fears of rejection and abandonment begin to diminish. Rebirth may be the best word to describe the transformation, for the love received is truly like water irrigating the soil from which will come the flower: the true self as originally envisaged by God in his creation. Hidden talents begin to emerge in the new atmosphere of loving reverence built up by spiritual union.

For me the most precious gift of union in spiritual friendship is the foretaste of heaven it gives. Its very nature is to be everlasting, without end in time, and this in itself is so rare as to be a hint of the unending, unlimited way we will experience all the joys of eternity.

Spiritual friendship is also a foretaste of heaven in another sense: in providing moments of timelessness, a feeling of being lifted above all time in pure wonder, saturated with love. This happens most often during times of prayer together.

We are not surprised that such experiences are real when we realize that true spiritual friendship has its roots in the will of Christ, as expressed in the quotation from the Gospel of Saint John at the beginning of this chapter. In heaven God will be the source of all our happiness, but he has willed that a concomitant joy will consist in participating in the holy beatitude of our friends.[55]

The impression should not be given that all suffering ends at the stage of union. There are times of anguish here just as during former phases. Yet these times feel different since they take place within the heart of Christ whose sweetness permeates them in a way difficult to describe to any who have not had the experience. Perhaps it can be compared to the way a parent is pierced by the pain of a child, yet simultaneously wants to be there because of their close bond. Identification with Christ makes sorrow for him and in him something desirable, even if dreadful.

Physical separation, even over long periods, of those united in spiritual friendship, brings yearning and sadness, but no longer has a depressing or despairing character, as it would in the enchantment period.

As the union grows, there may also be an agonized feeling of being suspended between heaven and earth, unable to consummate one's love in a physical way, yet unable to lift oneself into a purely angelic perspective because of one's humanity.

At times one may wonder why God gives the gift of so lofty a relationship only to thwart it by the interference of less lofty claims on time and energy.

What has come to me in prayer and meditation regarding the suspension ushered in by friendship of union is that we would not long for heaven unless God had given us so enormous a capacity for love. The imagination will one day attain its goal in the contemplation of the glory of the new heaven and new earth; while still in time, it practices, as it were, on whatever glimpses of its future state the present offers.

In the occasional times of temptation that come even at this stage, we must remember that God who made us knows our weakness after the Fall. He will give the grace to love in a holy manner. It is he who has made such friendship, not to be a tidbit of a forbidden romance, but to be a true foretaste of heaven where there will be no giving in marriage.

A wise woman once wrote me a letter about spiritual friendship, indicating a sensible path for the increase of union and the avoidance of pitfalls. I admire the simplicity of her approach:

> Keep your friendship outward reaching and giving and loving of others so that it does not become too self-engrossed. Focus on God and not on each other. Set guidelines for your friendship, and be aware of possible dangers. Remind each other from time to time of what you want from your friendship and what you do not want.

> Keep your separateness; allow each other to develop according to your own pace. Remember that love is a gift. Rejoice in what you have, not in what must never be. Keep your priorities in prudent, proper focus. Laugh about any minor problems that arise, and do better next time. Be caught up in the person, not the passion. Bring God and prayer to your meetings always. Do not ever give bad example.

Over-dependency may also arise as a difficulty in the union phase. St. John of the Cross wrote that when two take a path, at some point they will each have to travel their own way. It is as if God were occasionally to step between the two and hold them at arm's length, or to make them touch fingertips instead of holding hands.

What is beautiful about union in friendship is that such times of greater distance will always be accepted, no matter how painful, for the friends can find each other in prayer where the apex of each soul is in touch with Christ.

Before giving contemporary instances of union in spiritual friendship, and excerpts from the lives and writings of the saints, I wish to append here two short poems of my own and a longer one by a dear friend.

Spiritual Friendship
a flickering altar candle
serviced by angelic sacristans?
Catholic trumpery?
Only if God is *not* love!

———

Swathed in grace
muted song
not fire
but light
not fantasy
but reality
Thanks be to God.

———

Love's Radiant Light
by Dianne Miller

Brilliance more blinding than noonday sun,
   Radiant Light, Light of my life,
   Enlightening my own.
Source of all light,
   Light Itself has shone
   Inflaming with Its Light
   All It shines upon.

Body barriers broken,
   My spirit by This Light
   set free!
Yearning with burning desire,
   My spirit cries out
   For consummation in
   Light's Loving Fire eternally.

Before my own another light shines,
  My dear friend's own spirit
    Radiates the image
    I've seen of my God—
    Love's Light beholding.

In hope-filled abandonment
  My spirit stretches out
    To the light that is my friend,
        Spirit embracing God
        In the gift of knowing him.

As closer I come to him
  Light's enlightenment reveals
    What I recognize in my friend
        Is my own true self;
    Spirit reflecting God's Image
        In him, mirroring my own
        For me to see.

His love for God
    Drew me on...and beyond
        Any embrace for myself
    Save for me,
        God's Own.

My own spirit's light
  Passed through my friend's own,
    A moment of union
        In God's Light,
        Our lights shone
        As one.

Then beyond embrace of clinging
  In a blinding flash
    All light in

God's Own Light
Bursting!

Magnificent Obsession
  Light's Own possession,
    Spirit unto spirit
      Alone in God
      All light
      All friends
        In God's embracing Love
        Eternally in Light
        Shine forth
        In union, as One.

Some of the most beautiful spiritual friendships of our century have been enjoyed by married couples. They would have been great friends in Christ even had they not been married, but the intimacy of their life together, day by day, makes their stories different from those of partners who see each other only in special circumstances.

The couple whose story I will relate shared a common profession and worked side by side at it even before they were married. An older couple, they had no children.

Every morning they would arise, say a morning prayer together and go to Mass. During the Liturgy, observers would watch a real spiritual sharing going on between them. They knew each other's thoughts so well that an exchange of glances would acknowledge that this particular phrase from Scripture was a favorite of the other person.

Devoted to the apostolate, much of their daily conversation centered on ways of reaching others for Christ, or of discerning God's will in the difficult practical aspects of decision-making. Twilight found them praying Vespers together; in the evening they listened to music, and then prayed Compline before retiring.

As the man died many years before the woman, the widow's grief was overwhelming because the two had lived together as twin-souls. After some years, however, she was able to experience his presence in a strong and abiding manner. The reality of that spiritual presence was so great that everyone who visited her felt they had been communing with his spirit as well.

A lay contemplative living in the world had a cloistered nun as one of his spiritual friends. He visited her five times a year at her convent where they would speak together about the wonder of God and of Christ's love in the Church. Their eyes would sparkle with joy and a certain atmosphere of happiness surrounded them as they spoke.

In between visits, the contemplative would write the nun meditative articles about the Psalms, the Song of Songs and other Scripture passages. He also wrote to her of his love for her soul, encouraging her to see how his own love for her reflected Christ's joy in her beauty.

The relationship reached its peak when the nun was dying, most painfully, of cancer. At the time of her drawn out suffering, she could feel the holy love of her friend sharing the agony with her. She would reassure him that her first act in heaven would be to ask that he come soon to join her.

This was not to be, for he lived many years afterward, but the fragrance of their love remained to inspire the other nuns in the convent, as well as the man's lay friends. Many of the articles he wrote first to her were to be published over the years for the edification of others in the Church.

What wonderful things the saints have to say about spiritual union. I will never forget the first time I read the Gospel of St. John when I was twenty years old. Brought up as a complete atheist, I found the other Gospel accounts interesting and intriguing, but most strange, for I was so unfamiliar with anything supernatural. When I read St. John, even though the atmosphere of the book was still more other-worldly, I felt transported into the mystery of Christ by the mystical light of John's words. The model of the spiritual union is that of Mary, Joseph and Jesus, but we find another model in that of John's relationship with his Savior. Asked whether Jesus did not also love the other disciples, since John called himself the beloved one, a commentator sagely replied: Of course, Jesus loved all the apostles and disciples, but perhaps John was one who appreciated the intimacy of that love in a special way.

Some of the most beautiful passages about the union of spiritual friends are to be found in Aelred's writings. Speaking of Ivo, a beloved friend who had died, the Cistercian Abbot wrote:

> Yes, his constant love and affection are, in fact, always so fresh to my mind, that, though he has gone from this life in body, yet to my spirit he seems never to have died at all. For there he is ever with me, there his pious countenance inspires me, there his charming eyes smile upon me, there his happy words have such relish for me, that either I seem to have gone to a better land with him or he seems still to be dwelling with me here on earth.[56]

> The day before yesterday, as I was walking the round of the cloister of the monastery, the brethren were sitting around forming as it were a most loving crown. In the midst...of the delights of paradise with the leaves, flowers and fruits of each single tree, I marveled. In that multitude of brethren I found no one whom I did not love, and no one by whom, I felt sure, I was not loved. I was filled with such joy that it surpassed all the

delights of this world. I felt, indeed, my spirit transfused into all and the affection of all to have passed into me, so that I could say with the Prophet: "Behold, how good and how pleasant it is for brethren to dwell together in unity" (Ps 132:1).[57]

...A friend, praying to Christ on behalf of his friend, and for his friend's sake desiring to be heard by Christ, directs his attention with love and longing to Christ. Then it sometimes happens that quickly and imperceptibly the one love passes over into the other, and coming, as it were, into close contact with the sweetness of Christ himself, the friend begins to taste his sweetness and to experience his charm. Thus ascending from that holy love with which he embraces a friend to that with which he embraces Christ, he will joyfully partake in abundance of the spiritual fruit of friendship, awaiting the fullness of all things in the life to come... [when] this friendship, to which here we admit but few, will be outpoured upon all and by all outpoured upon God, and God shall be all in all.[58]

St. Bernard tells us to rest in those we love, for "creatures are so many rays emanating from the sun Christ is, giving us a hint of all God is."[59]

On one of those rare occasions when St. Francis visited Clare in her convent, he took along a group of the brothers. It is said that the people of Assisi were alarmed to see the convent on fire, only to discover that this flame was a mystical sign of the love the brothers and sisters had for each other in Christ.

Of St. Teresa of Avila, Mother Mary Clare Vincent,

OSB, writes: "Friendship for Teresa is also an important symbol of our relationship to the Divine. She begins the *Way of Perfection* by saying that since Christ has so many enemies and so few friends, these few should be good ones. Then, almost immediately, she states the characteristics of good human friendship: detachment, trust, fidelity, selflessness, honesty and freedom. Divine love is the same. Later on she relates friendship back to God. In Chapter 26 of the *Way of Perfection,* she urges her nuns to seek a friend, and advises them to choose Christ. 'Do you think it's some small matter to have a friend like this at your side?' she asks *(Way,* 26.1). And in Chapter 32 she writes that as we grow in union with God, 'he begins to commune with the soul in so intimate a friendship that he not only gives it back its own will but gives it his. For in so great a friendship the Lord takes joy in putting the soul in command, as they say, and he does what it asks since it does his will'" *(Way,* 32.23).[60]

St. John of the Cross teaches that the "soul knows creatures through God and not God through creatures."[61]

In his *Treatise on the Love of God,* St. Francis de Sales writes: "When we see our neighbor, created in the image and likeness of God, should we not say to one another, 'Stop, do you see this created being, do you see how it resembles the Creator?' Should we not cast ourselves upon him, caress him, weep over him with love? Should we not give him a thousand blessings?..."[62]

At one time Therese of Lisieux thought it was far better not to have had the consolations of friendship. Later on she wrote about the union of two in God as a reward for years of detachment.[63] Therese's thought may be considered as part of a growing tendency among spiritual writers to consider the blessings of friendship in Christ so great that such friendship should be recommended to all Christians striving to live a devout life. Fr. Lacordaire (1802-61) wrote that "true friendship is a rare and divine thing, a sure mark of a noble soul and one of the greatest rewards of true virtue."[64] "There is nothing so precious as a faithful friend" (Sir. 6:15).

I would like to end with quotations from letters of Charles Rich, a contemplative author of several books about spirituality.[65]

"Love is the food of the soul. In heaven we will live on the food that love for Christ is."

"Just as people wanting to climb a high mountain tie a rope around each other so if one falls the other holds him up, so it is with spiritual friendship on the road to heaven."

When friends complain about being separated on earth they should remember "if we had heaven on earth it would be a pseudo kind of bliss and not the kind they enjoy who have had the grace to depart from this life, seeing that true love, the one Christ is, has to be accompanied by pain, since it is with pain alone that we can sanctify our immortal souls. There is a yearning to now in this life become what we will be in the one to come, and it is this yearning God wants us to have... it is He who is responsible for the joy of heart derived from knowing and loving our friends."

"It is our friend as she will be in heaven that we love, the one who will live forever."

"What bliss Adam and Eve experienced in their relationship with each other before they sinned! By loving Christ in the way all the saints have loved him, we can re-experience the joys had by our first parents before they sinned, love for Christ enabling us to regain the joys had by Adam before he sinned."

"In a way, I don't miss your [his friend's] physical presence, for God has given me the grace to have you in the substance of the soul, because you are there always with me, and this more vividly than when I see you. You have become such an inseparable part of my own inner being that these two inner beings are now one in the way they will be after this life is over.

"In a way, this life *is* over in part, for the real me is now in heaven as is the real you, by means of prayer and by means of the love we have for each other in Christ the Lord. It is in that immortal state I have placed your dear self, to be kept safe for all eternity."

May each of us experience such union in our friendships, through Christ our Lord, now and for all eternity, for God is Love.

Notes

1. Dietrich von Hildebrand, *Man and Woman* (Chicago: Franciscan Herald Press, 1965), p. 69.

2. *The Benedictine Bulletin:* St. Scholastica's Priory Letter (Petersham, MA: St. Bede's Publications, Spring, 1986).

3. Cf. Ambrose, St., "Duties for a Clergy" *(The Nicene Fathers,* II).

4. St. (Abbot) Aelred of Rievaulx' *Spiritual Friendship* translated by Sr. Mary Eugenia Laker, SSND, with an introduction by Douglass Roby (Kalamazoo, Michigan: Cistercian Publications, 1977).

5. Ibid., p. 18.

6. Ibid., p. 53.

7. Ibid., p. 92.

8. Ibid., p. 19.

9. Cf. *The Life of St. Francis of Assisi* (London: Longman, Green and Co., 1948), pp. 160-161.

10. Conleth Kearns, OP, translator and author of introduction, *The Life of St. Catherine of Siena* (Wilmington, Delaware: Michael Glazier, Inc., 1980).

11. Notre Dame, Indiana: Ave Maria Press, 1974.

12. *The Collected Works of St. Teresa of Avila,* Vol. I, Kavanaugh and Rodriguez, translators (Washington, DC: ICS Publications, 1976).

13. Ibid., p. 58ff.

14. Ibid., p. 47.

15. From *The Imitation of Christ* by Thomas a Kempis (Milwaukee: The Bruce Publishing Company, 1940), p. 13. Reprinted with permission of Macmillan Publishing Company.

16. *The Collected Works of St. Teresa of Avila,* Vol. I, pp. 64-65.

17. *Imitation of Christ,* p. 163.

18. Ibid., p. 189.

19. For details of this friendship, see the book about St. Francis of Sales: *The Gentleman Saint* by Margaret Trouncer (London: The Catholic Book Club, 1963).

20. Ibid., p. 176.

21. Excerpt from *Introduction to the Devout Life* by St. Francis de

Sales, translation by John K. Ryan, translation copyright 1950 by Harper & Brothers. Used by permission of Doubleday, a division of Bantam Doubleday Dell Publishing Group, Inc. Also used with permission of the Society for the Propagation of the Faith.

22. Ibid., XIX.

23. Ibid.

24. *Elizabeth Seton—Selected Writings,* edited by Ellin Kelly and Annabelle Melville (New York: Paulist Press, 1987).

25. From *Studies in Formative Spirituality,* Vol. II, no. 1, February 1981, p. 79.

26. *The Ascent of Mount Carmel,* in *The Collected Works of St. John of the Cross,* Kavanaugh and Rodriguez, translators (Washington, DC: ICS Publications, 1979), p. 98.

27. Vol. II, *The Complete Works of St. Teresa,* Allison Peers, translator (London and New York: Sheed and Ward, 1957), pp. 21-34.

28. See, for example, Joseph I. Dirvin, CM, *Mrs. Seton* (New York: Farrer, Strauss and Cudahy, 1962).

29. Petersham, MA: St. Bede's Publications, 1984.

30. Cf. *De Beatitudine caelestis.* P.L. clix 638, Minge.

31. *The Way of Perfection,* Chapter 7, in Vol. II, *The Complete Works of St. Teresa,* Allison Peers, translator (London and New York: Sheed & Ward, 1957).

32. *The Collected Works of St. Teresa of Avila,* Vol. I, p. 282.

33. The letters were published by Allison Peers with Newman Press, 1950. The article about them is in *Spiritual Life,* Volume 29, Number 3, Fall, 1983.

34. *The Ascent of Mount Carmel,* in *The Collected Works of St. John of the Cross,* Book II, Chapter 22, 11-12, p. 183.

35. Aelred, *Spiritual Friendship,* pp. 80-81.

36. St. Ambrose on his brother, Satryus.

37. *Man and Woman,* pp. 69-70.

38. *Introduction to the Devout Life,* pp. 125-126.

39. *Edith Stein: A Biography* by Waltraud Herbstrith, translated by Fr. Bernard Bonowitz. Copyright © 1971 by Verlagsgessellschaft Gerhard Kaffke mbh, Ashaffenburg. English Translation © 1985 by Harper & Row, Publishers, Inc., Chapter 14.

40. *C. S. Lewis's Case for the Christian Faith* by Richard L. Purtill. © 1981 by Richard L. Purtill, Harper & Row, Publishers, Inc., pp. 97-98.

41. *The Way of Perfection,* p. 176.

42. Ibid., p. 17ff.

43. Ibid., p. 87.

44. *The Collected Works of St. Teresa of Avila,* Vol I, p. 128.

45. *The Dark Night,* in *The Collected Works of St. John of the Cross,* Book I, Chapter 4, 6-7, p. 305.

46. *Introduction to the Devout Life,* pp. 120-121.

47. See *The Story of St. Francis de Sales* by Katherine Bregy. Milwau-

kee: The Bruce Publishing Company, 1958. Reprinted with permission of Macmillan Publishing Company.

48. Archives of St. Joseph's Provincial House, X, 10, Seton to Filicchi, Winter 1805-6.

49. Excerpt from *The Ascent to Truth* by Thomas Merton, copyright 1951 by The Abbey of Our Lady of Gethsemane and renewed 1979 by The Trustees of the Merton Legacy Trust, reprinted by permission of Harcourt Brace Javanovich, Inc., p. 165.

50. New York: Paulist Press, 1985.

51. Whitinsville, MA: Affirmation Books, 1980.

52. *Introduction to the Devout Life*, pp. 127-128.

53. *Spiritual Friendship*, pp. 62-63.

54. New York: Seabury Press: Copyright 1981 by Donald Nicholl, p. 116. Reprinted by permission of Harper & Row, Publishers, Inc.

55. See Thomas Aquinas: *Summa Theologica*, I, II, Q. 4, article, Great Books, Vol 19, p. 636.

56. *Spiritual Friendship*, p. 70.

57. Ibid., 112.

58. Ibid., pp. 131-132.

59. Cf. Commentary on the Song of Songs.

60. *The Benedictine Bulletin*: St. Scholastica's Priory Letter (Petersham, MA: St. Bede's Publications, Spring, 1986).

61. *The Living Flame of Love*, in *The Collected Works of St. John of the Cross*, stanza 4: 5.

62. *Introduction to the Devout Life*, p. 172.

63. Cf. *Autobiography* (Kennedy edition, Soeur Therese version, pp. 143, 158).

64. Quoted in *Spiritual Theology* by Jordan Aumann, OP (Kansas City: Sheed and Ward), p. 378 ff.

65. See *The Embrace of the Soul* (Petersham, MA: St. Bede's, 1984) and *Reflections*, also published by St. Bede's.

St. Paul Book & Media Centers

ALASKA

750 West 5th Ave., Anchorage, AK 99501 907-272-8183.

CALIFORNIA

3908 Sepulveda Blvd., Culver City, CA 90230 310-397-8676.

1570 Fifth Ave. (at Cedar Street), San Diego, CA 92101 619-232-1442

46 Geary Street, San Francisco, CA 94108 415-781-5180.

FLORIDA

145 S.W. 107th Ave., Miami, FL 33174 305-559-6715; 305-559-6716.

HAWAII

1143 Bishop Street, Honolulu, HI 96813 808-521-2731.

ILLINOIS

172 North Michigan Ave., Chicago, IL 60601 312-346-4228; 312-346-3240.

LOUISIANA

4403 Veterans Memorial Blvd., Metairie, LA 70006 504-887-7631; 504-887-0113.

MASSACHUSETTS

50 St. Paul's Ave., Jamaica Plain, Boston, MA 02130 617-522-8911.

Rte. 1, 885 Providence Hwy., Dedham, MA 02026 617-326-5385.

MISSOURI

9804 Watson Rd., St. Louis, MO 63126 314-965-3512; 314-965-3571.

NEW JERSEY

561 U.S. Route 1, Wick Plaza, Edison, NJ 08817 908-572-1200.

NEW YORK

150 East 52nd Street, New York, NY 10022 212-754-1110.

78 Fort Place, Staten Island, NY 10301 718-447-5071; 718-447-5086.

OHIO

2105 Ontario Street (at Prospect Ave.), Cleveland, OH 44115 216-621-9427.

PENNSYLVANIA

214 W. DeKalb Pike, King of Prussia, PA 19406 215-337-1882; 215-337-2077.

SOUTH CAROLINA

243 King Street, Charleston, SC 29401 803-577-0175.

TEXAS

114 Main Plaza, San Antonio, TX 78205 512-224-8101.

VIRGINIA

1025 King Street, Alexandria, VA 22314 703-549-3806.

CANADA

3022 Dufferin Street, Toronto, Ontario, Canada M6B 3T5 416-781-9131.